BECOME YOUR OWN HERO AGAIN

BY LEONARD SEKYONDA

Sekyonda Publishing.

1 Introduction

The Goal

I was 9 years old when I first got the news about my father passing away. I remember it like it was yesterday. It was my best friend's 10th birthday, and I was having a great day playing tag. The weather was great. We were all laughing until I was abruptly interrupted by my mother calling for me to come in. Why would she call me in when I was having so much fun? When I got inside my uncle was next to her and he asked me if I needed a drink, which I declined. He asked me again, and I replied, "I just said, I'm fine." They both looked at me as if they were trying to explain through their eyes something their mouths could not express. I remember thinking in my head, "Damn I'm missing out on so much fun out there." Up until that point my Dad had been ill and in and out of the hospital, so I remember scanning my brain to think about what their eyes could possibly be trying to say but their mouths couldn't. Like that, I said, "My dad has died, hasn't he?" They looked at me shocked and stunned. My mother responded, "How do you know?" I said, "It's fine, can I please go back to my friend's birthday." They looked at me surprised and I proceeded to go back out and join my friends. Little did I know the impact this loss would have on my life for both good and bad.

* * *

I was raised by my mother, a single parent who sacrificed the little she had to raise her two children. Though the low-income council housing system was struck on by poverty and gang violence, with her love and sheer strength we had a sense that we could be more. My mother use to drive us to school in a van every day and I would lay in the back - as the front only had two seats which my younger sister would occupy. However, no matter the situation, every morning while driving us in the van my mother would chant "We will always make it." and make us join in. It was our first introduction to positive incantations. There was was something about when we would all say it - a sense of possibilities and the idea that our situation was only temporary. She knowing or unknowingly instilled this belief into us that no matter the situation, we "will" always make it. As I got older, like all teenage boys, our relationship slightly drifted as I began my mission to discover myself. Although I made it to college, the sheer fact of the reality was that I needed to generate income as soon as possible. I took on a part-time job, but eventually the two clashed and my results began to take a hit. College is a very vital time in a teenagers' life and I slowly began to feel myself doubt who I was or what I was capable of based on my grades. All until one day when a colleague at my part-time job suggested I read a book. It was through this book that I discovered my full capability and the endless opportunities that the world still had for me.

Over the past few years, I have had to re-develop and recreate myself to progress and develop past my slang speaking, small-minded, and self-limiting mindset. The life-changing book that sparked all of this and my initial introduction to the world of personal development was through a book called *"Rich Dad Poor Dad."* The book was not only the first impactful and life-changing book I read but it was also essential to my initial development because it was the first book that offered me a new perspective on life. Growing up in South London, the options and examples of success were limited; sell drugs, play football, or make music AKA MC (which at the time made no money) - and I know this because I tried. To get a job at a corporate company, you had to have A's in Maths to even get an interview.

However, *Rich Dad Poor Dad* offered a different perspective. It spoke to me differently, like no other book ever had, because it suggested a possibility - that I had an option to be successful. It ignored my background, race, and upbringing, and simply provided an option which up until that point, I had never been given. That option was to control my destiny and create my wealth and success. School has a way of isolating your life options, especially when your grades are not going as well as you would want. It was refreshing to read something that allowed me to change and question my perspective. I believe that perspective has a lot to do with people and their relationship with success. What makes a 16-year-old teenager start an online business which he can then sell for hundreds of millions? What makes a 36-year-old man who still takes the train to work for 30K a year keep going in day after day? It's perspective!

* * *

While I was building the *MYCOMEUP.com* blog in the early years of 2009, one of the things we were known for was highlighting the stories of successful people from around the world. These included iconic sports figures and entrepreneurs such as Mike Tyson, Simon Cowell, 50 Cent, and more. However, while researching these figures before we posted about them, I noticed one thing they all had in common, and this was that they had all faced major setbacks in their personal and professional lives. Mike Tyson was from the ghettos of Brooklyn where his mother was a prostitute, leaving him to fend for himself and his siblings as a child. Simon Cowell went bankrupt, and 50 Cent was shot over 9 times just after signing his first record deal.

* * *

This was one of the keys behind the success of *MYCOMEUP.com,* and what set us apart from other sites as we wouldn't just highlight the progress of people, but also the painful journeys behind their stories. One common trait we all share as humans is the ability to empathize. We can find common ground through pain. Pain has a way of neutralizing our external perception of someone and creating more of an understanding and at times an appreciation for someone's success. When we understand the pain that someone has experienced, we link it to our situation. Through that link, our perspective changes and new ideas begin to form. You might start to think, "Maybe I can still do it." The goal of this book is to change your perspective and self-image. None of the people we admire are superheroes; they are humans like you and me who simply applied themselves and adopted many of the principles mentioned in this book.

Become Your Own Hero Again

In a time where social media is taking control of our social interactions, we are quickly becoming a generation more obsessed with idolizing the lives of others instead of building on our current strengths and weaknesses. We quickly lose our self-value and replace it with external acceptance - *likes, approvals,* and *comments*. The ability to see oneself is the ability to take time to look at our reflection - how we feel, and what our purpose is. Our reflection is our nakedness before the world can interact. This is why we must value falling in love with our reflections.

* * *

This book is more than a self-help book; it has been created to challenge the limiting perceptions we have in ourselves while exploring some of my business experiences in setting up and running my first international business in South Asia. The book provides principles and practices on building more self-value. The ultimate goal is to challenge limiting beliefs while redirecting the values you already have inside of you back to you.

2 Perception is Reality

The aim of *Become Your Own Hero Again* is to expand your perception so that you can snap out of the limitations that social conditioning ingrains in us. As a kid, our minds were extremely flexible. We had dreams of becoming astronauts, musicians, athletes, or whatever it was our hearts desired. Eventually, our surroundings started to break us down and tell us who we ought to be. Being a good student is no longer the fast track to success. More and more jobs are becoming automated, and it is the people with a creative spirit that will be able to thrive in the technological landscape since computers/robots will be able to do almost anything except for coming up with original ideas. The creative innovators who leverage the power of technology will benefit the most when the business world is transformed by artificial intelligence and automation. The naivety and curiosity that comes with being a child should be embraced. Remember how you felt as a kid, the creativity and spontaneity that came with youth. A playful attitude towards the world will broaden your horizons as the opportunities are limitless. Hang onto that playful naivety and do what you want to do.

3 Self-Acceptance

"God grant me the serenity to accept the things I cannot change, the courage to change the things I can and wisdom to know the difference"

– Serenity Prayer

Self-acceptance begins by coming to terms with who we are and facing uncomfortable truths about ourselves. It is only through brutal honesty that we can accept our life situation for better and for worse before moving forward. In general, our life situation is a byproduct of our choices, habits, and mindsets. If we look in the mirror and analyze our physique, whether we are in shape or not is a result of our past habits. We might have the urge to flex our body or stand differently in lighting so that we can appear more attractive to ourselves; we all play these little tricks on ourselves to feel better about who we are; the lies we tell ourselves to protect our ego. This self-deceit can manifest in many forms, for example, whether we take responsibility for our finances or how we treat the people around us.

Identity

I was 20 years old when I first started my business in the Philippines. Initially, I used an alias because

I didn't want to show my face, and I used my middle name as my last name, as I knew my last name would reveal that I'm black. My thoughts were if I make my name Leonard Emmanuel instead of Leonard Sekyonda, and made my profile picture of a white guy, it would prevent negative stereotypes from holding me back. While working with these companies, they wanted me to come over to the Philippines. They wanted to run a FaceTime and see a photo of me so they could market me. I was scared that sharing a picture of me could hinder my deal. I thought that they would figure out that I was a young black kid and they wouldn't want to do business with me. I had a few days to think about which photo to share. It felt more comfortable to share my display picture, a nerdy looking white guy. However, they would eventually have to see me, and I didn't have the money to send a stunt double over instead! I had a nice picture of myself from when I was at SkyBar in Los Angeles a few months earlier - a proud milestone for me. Even though I was broke and sleeping on a couch at the time, the photo looked super inspiring; I was wearing shades and looked more like an actor than a businessman.

Covering my eyes, I gripped my mouse and nervously clicked the send button. There was a slight pause, and I watched anxiously as they typed a response. To my surprise, I lifted my head to an answer that read, "Oh my god, you are so handsome; you look like Will Smith." It was at that time that I realized that I had almost allowed my insecurities to prevent me from not only developing my business but on a deeper level it uncovered that I had not accepted who I am. I didn't see the value in my human ability. The concept of self-acceptance works in two ways; in the physical and psychological. I had allowed the psychological concept of my race and age, and the theory of both being a disadvantage almost prevented me from seeing value in myself. I allowed the stereotype of a middle-aged white businessman to be more acceptable than me. Not to forget the fact that I have convinced myself in my heart that I was 90% sure they would not want to work with me after sending my true identity. This is an example from my personal life where a limiting belief around skin color and age almost prevented me from following through on a goal. After this, it became evident that the world was accepting me before I was.

Eventually, people only care about your

deliverables. Are you reliable at sticking with the things you commit to? I started to realize that it's a bad long-term strategy to assume that I needed to hide behind another face because I was young or black. People may be biased with age, gender, or race, but ultimately it's our deliverables that define us in the business world. People may have biases in the beginning, but if you can prove them wrong by being effective in what you do, then that is ultimately going to be the mark for you as an individual. In the end, your reputation will speak for itself, and you will be setting the terms in business because they need your business more than you need theirs. We all have our flaws and our regrets. We are only human after all. All of the negative stories that exist in our psyche are normal and are a fundamental part of the human experience. This doesn't mean we have to suffer as a result of our past experiences. Only by acknowledging that we have been untrue to our highest self that we can start to come into alignment with our values. Our mistakes exist as a teacher, the lessons of the past that prepare us for the future. The feeling of regret can weigh us down and hold us back. Often, the feeling stays with us until we have spent long enough processing the experience so that we can learn from it and avoid self-harm from the same mistakes going forward.

You can't afford to carry the pain of the past around with you. It should only be carried on long enough for it to teach you lessons. The traumas of the past don't necessarily heal overnight, but there is harm in living a lifestyle of avoidance. Acknowledge the parts of yourself that are in pain, accept that the pain is there, and make a commitment to becoming the best version of yourself.

4 Failure

In the real world, failure lasts only as long as the sentence. It's only a failure when the word failure is ascribed to a situation. Failure is a transient experience. The process of chasing down a goal and the engagement of the journey itself is what gives our experiences sentimental value. Go after what you love if it means enough to you.

"When we succeed, we party. When we fail, we ponder."

– Anthony Robbins

When we strive to reach our goals, sometimes we win and sometimes we lose – when we lose we are blessed with a lesson to learn from so that we can come back stronger the next time around. Failure is not a catastrophe; it is a feedback. It gives us new information to take back to the drawing board so that we can adjust our strategies. The average millionaire *fails* three times before hitting their *home run* that makes them their fortune. In a sense, the learning lesson from this is to fail fast and fail often. If you can avoid failure by learning from others and embracing planning and preparation – excellent. Don't waste time worrying about failure and letting it paralyze you.

It can help to view failures as experiments instead. Did Thomas Edison fail on 10,000 designs before inventing the light bulb or did he experiment 10,000 times? If he allowed himself to be defeated by the first few setbacks on his journey, then he wouldn't have invented the light bulb. The process of doing, gathering feedback and then optimizing the process is key to success.

5 Rock Bottom

Hitting *rock bottom* can be a catalyst for some of the greatest changes that take place in our lifetime. Times of desperation give us clarity if we are open to them. Ego shattering events allow us to notice when we have been living in a haze and ignoring our heart's deepest desires. The feeling of hitting *rock bottom* is not necessarily a catastrophe, things can only get better if you have indeed hit *rock bottom*. When things do get overwhelming, it's important to pay attention in these moments, of course, to mitigate the chances of things getting worse by not making impulsive decisions - these moments of desperation give us wisdom. We get to see what is important to us when we feel as though we have lost everything. We start to analyze our behavior patterns and determine what is truly meaningful to us. Some people say, there are only two things that make people change - *inspiration* or *desperation*. Usually, it is desperation. Feelings of desperation can be used to accelerate change throughout your life. Embrace the feelings of desperation because they are very much a normal part of the human experience - it's nothing to be ashamed of.

Accountability can function as a powerful means of combating bad habits. Working with friends and mentors and committing to making changes can work as a powerful force when creating the life you desire. Many of us don't mind letting ourselves down when it comes to our habits, because our decisions are based around what we want to do at the moment, but the added pressure of our peers often forces us to be more long-term minded.

Be the hero of your own story!

We are not defined by our past; we are prepared by it. Look deep within yourself and have time to think. Let the thoughts come through you. In silence, we can genuinely face ourselves. Negative thoughts will come through; the things we avoid will surface eventually. Majority of us live in a state of perpetual distraction, by using social media, work, food and other forms of instant gratification. These kinds of distractions exist as a means of escaping from the thoughts that make us uncomfortable. It is hugely important for everyone to face their demons. Repression and avoidance will eventually lead to a need for more intense forms of distraction which are ultimately self-destructive and take away from our capacity to experience higher levels of self-awareness and consciousness. A lifestyle of avoidance only becomes more difficult as we are using pleasure and dopamine spikes as a Band-Aid for past traumas, which can be a precursor for addiction. This is why so many people make millions, only to ruin their life through an excess of sex and drugs. By acknowledging the existence of the pain hiding deep down, we can avoid the downward spirals that come from a life of immediate gratification.

True strength, power, and well-being come from the ability to face our emotions in their fullest form.

The best way to come back from regret is to set higher ideals and make yourself accountable since you are now blessed with a higher level of consciousness that comes with life experience. Being honest with ourselves will make our lives easier in the long run. The sooner we can be real with ourselves, the sooner we can begin healing ourselves on a deep spiritual level. When we heal ourselves, it makes it easier for us to love and heal others.

6 Self-Belief

Everybody has a moment in their life where they have to decide whether or not they will make the change. A lot of the time, what we miss out on, is remembering that it is us that makes that decision at the moment. People are supposed to be around us to elevate us and help us grow, but if we take it back to that moment where we made a pivotal decision, it creates a significant shift in self that we must take ownership of because it is that shift that enables us to believe in whether or not we are capable of meeting the challenge. We use the word *self* because before anyone gets in the picture before someone can give us feedback and help us, we need to understand that our decision creates the reality we are about to manifest for ourselves and the people we draw into our network. So, the real question that needs to be addressed when it comes to self-belief is to understand whether or not we decided to create the destiny we are striving for. Our self-belief is often determined by how much energy we exert towards honoring our decision.

Dave Chappelle, at the age of 14 was going to comedy clubs with his mother, and at that age, decided he was going to make a living as a comic. His talent and passion shined through, and he had suddenly monetized his craft at an early age. He had made the decision to honor his brand and his craft. He wanted to maintain integrity around the comedy that he found funny, not necessarily what the mainstream appreciated. He was offered a contract for $30 million dollars, which is an enormous amount especially for the world of comedy. Chappelle decided to reject the offer, deciding there were more important things to him in life, and ended up taking a break to go live in Africa. He then made a return back to comedy and people were still talking about how he walked away from the $30 million dollar deal only for him to later receive a contract which he accepted coming in at $60 million dollars because it was in alignment with his values. Chappelle knew what his beliefs were and stuck to them. In the long run, it worked to his advantage and he was able to maintain his integrity as an artist. The more we stay in alignment with our beliefs, the less the outside world can dictate what we see as possible.

7 Value Your Mind-Space

In the world of marketing, our attention functions as a commodity. Companies such as McDonalds and Coca-Cola pay exuberant amounts of money for just a few seconds of advertising during big events like the Super Bowl. They are paying for a moment of your subconscious. Our subconscious is impressionable enough for marketing industries to spend millions of dollars to show you products you are already aware of. It must work through -

why is Coca-Cola the default choice when we are ordering food? Is it the best drink? Or, is there a sense of familiarity around the brand that comes from our exposure to Coca-Cola advertising? Then what happens when we take control of it? What happens when we make a conscious effort around programming our psyche for the best possible life outcomes? This is what the main purpose of goal setting is. It's about taking control of the subconscious so that motivation and strategy are at the forefront of our reality.

So how do we tap into this power?

Write your goals down. The mere act of writing a goal down puts the wheels into motion. Your subconscious mind begins calculating a strategy for helping you get to where you want to be. In a sense, the universe starts to work for you.

The Reticular Activating System (RAS)

The Reticular Activating System (RAS) is located at the base of our brain. It functions as a means of processing and self-selecting information in our environment that is important. Our brains process over 6 million images per second. This is more than the conscious mind can handle. The RAS is there to select the images that it finds relevant to conscious and sub-conscious being. When we write our goals down, we enable ourselves to tap into all of our senses. The mind begins to visualize and believe what it is feeling and seeing. We become immersed in the future reality we wish to manifest.

8 Motion Creates Emotion

The upward spiral begins when we start taking care of ourselves. It is not unusual for us to feel stuck, especially if we have put all of our time into schooling when we are not enjoying it. Negative schooling experiences should not stop you from working on yourself. The simplest targets to aim for that produce measurable results in a short amount of time is getting to the gym or doing exercise.

* * *

Within a few months of lifting weights, you can transform your life in a big way. Losing weight and gaining muscle provide you with evidence that you can succeed and change the world when you put your mind into something. Having health and fitness commitments force discipline. This discipline then transfers into other areas of your life. For example, if you start going to the gym, you might start eating better food, meeting like-minded inspired people at the gym, and getting better sleep. These factors compound leaving you feeling more relaxed, focused, and determined. Little victories keep us motivated and make us addicted to winning. Small, realistic goals that can be achieved within a few months build momentum. Eventually, winning becomes instinctual even when the odds seem stacked against you.

9 Ways Social Media is Weakening Us

Social media is a powerful tool. We can connect and communicate with almost anyone in the world; it's like a superpower. But on the flip side, it's a great source of insecurity for the lots of people. Social media has created a landscape where on some level, every person that shares a post does it with the intention of receiving *likes* from the people around them. So, by default people are navigating a landscape of smoke and mirrors. People have filters on their photos, looking the best they possibly can, and perhaps subtly bragging about a lifestyle that they don't even live. For the average person that passively watches the *socialites* on social media platforms, a tremendous amount of inadequacy can come from comparing oneself with the more *successful* looking people. An even more terrible habit occurs in struggling individuals where they hate their own life so much that they would rather wake up to see what other people are doing when they should be focusing on improving their own life. People are handing their authority over to other people. They are losing sight of their tastes around what is cool or stylish and let social success in the form of *likes* function as a metric for success. This metric also hinders the creative experience by limiting our capacity to be unique if there is too much influence from others. If you are on social media and you aren't using it to grow your business, then you are being used by it. Take a step back from all that you see online. The intention behind social marketing is to make you feel less and instead redirect your confidence into needing to be supported by the use of their product. You are already complete and have everything you need for happiness; it's a matter of perspective.

10 Create Your New Picture

What is your ideal day five years from now?

In fiv years from now, who do you want to be? How does your perfect day unfold? Don't be afraid of making your goals and vision incredibly wild and detached from your everyday experience and perceptions. Who would you have to become so that you can see yourself in the best possible light? What would it take for you to feel your greatest sense of pride? At the same time, it is appreciation that helps us embrace where we are at. Perhaps you want the freedom to enjoy a simple lifestyle?

Imagine your ideal day, tap into all of your senses

An example of an ideal day five years from now might look like this:

I wake up and look over to my left; I see my beautiful wife. She is amazing. I am filled with a sense of appreciation for having such an amazing woman in my life.

I stand up and walk towards my wardrobe. I notice the Tom Ford spray scent. The perfume is triggered every time I step into my walk-in wardrobe. I see my line and suits. I don't pick any of them. I decide to go to the gym first. I put on my gym clothing instead. Everything is white, matches, and fits perfectly.

I go downstairs. There is a chef cooking breakfast. I can hear our gardener mowing the lawn. I walk out of the house and get inside my Ferrari 458. I take the top down. I start driving towards the gym and someone notices me. They tell me they love my work and to keep doing what I am doing. I arrive at the gym and work out with my trainer. He is one of the leading trainers in Los Angeles. I come out of the training feeling amazing, and my nutritionist is waiting for me with my meal prepared. I have a shower, then meet up with a friend for a coffee. He is talking about some international business and property deals that I should get involved in. I then get back in my car. Some more people recognize me and say to me they love what I do. I get home. My whole family is up. I have a few kids. They are all chirping. There is a barbecue going on. Some more friends have come over. I look up and notice it is one of those perfect days.

It is important that we place no limitations on our ideal day. We need to be imaginative. People often have problems thinking big about themselves. This is something that we need to break away from. The more limitations we have in our mind, the less we will be able to manifest in real life. If we choose a goal that truly compels us, then we should give ourselves a chance of reaching that target. With no targets, we approach stagnation. It is a good idea to do affirmations and visualization exercises each morning, especially on weekdays. Determine what you want your life to look like. Each week review your goals as well. It is normal for your goals to change over time. Don't be surprised if you are modifying them every few weeks or months.

Family

We can be so focused on our mission that we forget the importance of our family and relationships. Our sense of well-being is tied very closely to how much love we are sharing with the people we care about. Being around the people we love has a healing effect on our soul. The people that love us unconditionally allow us to reconnect with our values and our sense of belonging. If there are people you care about, do your best to look after them, even if it's a phone call to check up on them.

* * *

Create Goals

Create goals that relate to the following: Financial/ Family/ Lifestyle/ Health/ Career

Where do I want to be in the next one to two years? List three to five targets for each factor.

When setting goals, I like to break down my visions into five components. They include financials, family, lifestyle, health, and career.

Short-Term Goals

For each area, list 3-5 things you want to improve and achieve in the next 2-3 months. Once you determine your goals, consider the sacrifices and changes needed to bring you closer to your goals.

* * *

Example: Short-Term Financial Goals Setting

1) *Increase my monthly income to $3,000 per month*
2) *Have $3,000 liquid in savings*
3) *Invest $100 per month in a stock*

Long-Term Goals

List 3-5 things out of each area you want to improve and achieve in the next 1-2 years. It might look like this:

Example: Long-Term Financial Goals Setting

1) *$30,000 deposit for a house*
2) *$20,000 investment portfolio*
3) *Revenue streams generating over $10,000 per month*

Do the same for each other model and don't hold back.

* * *

Your Short-Term Goal List

Financial Goals

1)

2)

3)

4)

5)

Family Goals

1)

2)

3)

4)

5)

Things I will need to change / lose

1)

2)

3)

4)

5)

Lifestyle Goals

1)

2)

3)

4)

5)

Health Goals

1)

2)

3)

4)

5)

Career Goals

1)

2)

3)

4)

5)

Your Long-Term Goal List

Financial Goals

1)

2)

3)

4)

5)

Family Goals

1)

2)

3)

4)

5)

Things I will need to change / lose

1)

2)

3)

4)

5)

Lifestyle Goals

1)

2)

3)

4)

5)

Health Goals

1)

2)

3)

4)

5)

Career Goals

1)

2)

3)

4)

5)

This should leave you with a minimum of 15 goals which we can then turn into daily affirmations.

11 Setting Goals

The main challenge we face when setting goals is finding the strength within ourselves to think bigger. We can usually achieve more than we presently believe. As we start to gain momentum and experience from the little victories, we begin to understand our potential and lack of limitations.

"Watch your thoughts, for they become words.

Watch your words, for they become actions.

Watch your actions, for they become habits.

Watch your habits, for they become character.

Watch your character, for it will become your destiny." – Frank Outlaw

The words we use in our mind and put out into the world are mighty; this power requires us to treat our words with great respect. The biggest decisions that presidents make to change the world come from words. Impact throughout the world is a result of words. The biggest deals you will make will be made of words. This might seem like a boring way of looking at the world, but what we get from this is the opportunity to control reality by taking control of the language that happens in our mind. This can be from making conscious decisions to plan goals or to maintain transparency and become aware of our opportunities by using affirmations. Through the manifestations of language, the mind works as a co-creator of reality. You can be the author and dictator of your own story. Our goals can be ambitious and feel risky. There is more risk in not aiming high. The biggest regrets people face in old age and on their deathbeds is not being all they can be – getting to the end of their life, being new to retirement, only to realize that they had worked a job they didn't like for what felt like a lifetime.

The goals we set often demand that we become the highest version of ourselves. The right goals can elevate us; they often push us to strive for more and rid ourselves of negativity in its many forms – toxicity in food, relationships, and habits.

Reviewing our goals each week gives us clarity and reason behind the energy exerted each day – it's a fast track to depression feeling exhausted day in, day out with no end goal in mind.

There can only be upsides when you consciously set out to create the life of your dreams.

12 Affirmations

Affirmations are a powerful way for programming the RAS and subconscious mind to seek out what is needed when pursuing a goal. You can write your goals for the future down and replay it in your mind, so it feels real, or you can read it out loud, or both. Reading out loud sounds silly, but think about it; would you be too scared to say bad things that could happen out loud? Would you feel like you would be jinxing yourself? Would your fears start to come true? It can certainly feel that way. Talking out loud about your goals and the positive things that you want and expect can work as a powerful way of emotionally aligning yourself with your future goals. When we are truly inspired by our goals, they become an obsession, something we are meticulously crafting a way every day because we are so compelled by our vision. Issues with motivation and procrastination start to dissolve when you become acutely aware of what you want.

Affirm Daily your New Reality

One exercise that can be used to bring your goals closer to the forefront of your RAS is a daily written incantation of your goals. This is a mental exercise that can be applied before you start your day. The benefit of writing our affirmations down on a daily basis is that we begin to allow our subconscious minds to become at one with our goals while highlighting our senses to any opportunities surrounding them. Affirmation should always be written in the present tense. Every word should be written as if you have already achieved the goal. Allow the power of your imagination to run free. Visualize every element of your goals as you write them. Paint vivid pictures in your mind as you write them. How does it feel to complete your goals? What do you smell? What can you hear? Let go through this process and live through your affirmations.

Creating Your Affirmations

The first step is to take 3-4 of your short-term goals.

For example

1) *Increase my monthly income to $3,000 Per Month*
2) *Have $3,000 Liquid in savings*
3) *Invest $100 per month in a stock*

Then create a mini paragraph no longer than 3 lines which includes all three goals but written from a place of already having achieved them. *For example: Money comes to me frequently. I'm already making over $3,000 Per Month, my investment portfolio is generating a good return, and I'm already $3,000 Liquid. I feel amazing; I'm special!* This is your first Affirmation which you should write out a minimum of 3x times.

The next affirmation should include 1-2 year goals.

For example

1) *$30,000 deposit for a house*
2) *Family all have private healthcare paid for*
3) *Revenue streams generating over $10,000 per month*

Then do the same and write 3 lines which include all three goals but written from a place of already having achieved them. *For example: I'm amazing, I'm living in my new house feels incredible, all of my friends ask me for stock advice due to my portfolios' high performance and my family is healthy and well.* This should also be written out a minimum of 3x times.

* * *

In total, you should have 2 affirmation paragraphs which first include your short-term goals and then your long-term goals. The power of this exercise not only brings your subconscious into an active state before your day starts, but it also connects your emotions to the goals. Write your affirmation on your good days as well as your bad days. Treat them as a guideline to who you are becoming. Become comfortable with the change which is to come, and live through it every day in your mind until it becomes a reality.

"You will get all you want in life if you help enough other people get what they want."

– Zig Ziglar

* * *

Blind Faith

Trust the process. Put trust in the process and not logic. The mind is like a sponge – it soaks up information both good and bad. We can never question its ability. We subconsciously rely on it to protect us through both memory and instinct which are both things we can't see, feel, or logically explain. You see, by trusting the mind and feeding it your goals, you are watering a seed that has a cause and effect that neither the eye nor life may immediately see come to effect. However, it's crucial to trust it. It may be weeks, months, or even years before the seed purifies but never, and I mean never, stop watering it. Instant gratification is a concept taught in stories and movies. As you develop and invest time in your goals, some good and some bad things may occur both in your personal and work life. It is your job to keep watering your seed whatever the situation may be. The seed you water today, is not for tomorrow but for the day you forgot you had been watering it the whole time. Trust the process and invest in yourself daily by feeding your RAS with the right information.

When I was 19 years old, I had barely traveled and hardly had enough money to pay for the little room I was renting with my friend. However, every day as part of my affirmation I would write that *I frequently travel to amazing destinations*. At the time I was stuck in rainy London, and my surroundings were far from the affirmations I wrote out. However, what gradually happened is my senses towards the concept of traveling increased, and I somehow made friends with someone whose parents owned a place in Malta! To my surprise, one day, he offered me the chance to travel with him and stay at his parents' place for free. Moments like these stick out to me because I could never have imagined either opportunity or outcome, but I know that my consistency in writing about traveling played a part in drawing both the person and the situation into my awareness.

Our surroundings affect us more than we think!

There is an intuitive misconception that many of us carry which is that a *man is an island*. We tend to underestimate the influential power that our friends have over our reality – for better and for worse. Many of our behaviors, mindsets, and habits are often mirroring the people around us. Beyond this, even associating with the wrong kinds of people can affect your life negatively. You might have heard the saying that we are the average of the five people we hang out with the most. This might be a scary thought if most of your friends are addicted and poor. However, we can choose to surround ourselves with people who are ahead of us financially, physically, and emotionally. Look at the subtle influences in your life. Do they support you or are they taking away from your vitality? Perhaps there is someone you follow on YouTube that inspires you to take action and get organized, or you are finding yourself watching videos over and over that make you feel bad about yourself. Pay attention to the various forces and be willing to neglect everything that is slowing you down.

* * *

If we spend years around people who do nothing but take drugs and party, it's likely that that will become our life. We will start to take on the habits of the people around us. On the contrary, if we are spending our time around people that are focused on their health, building their life and giving back to society, it is likely that we will also be taking an active approach in improving our life over the years. The people we choose to spend our time around can make a world of difference in our life outcomes. I learned very quickly that my surroundings were a very big dictator to whether or not I succeeded independently or within the group. Surroundings are a defining factor; the people we listen to shape our values.

When I was a kid, I loved Taekwondo. On the day

of my first competition, it was revealed that my friends who I had been training with me had been stealing from the church hall, the place we had been training at. Because of this, we were not allowed to compete – just by associating with the wrong kinds of people, your opportunities can get restricted.

"Show me your friends, and I will show you your future."
– Dan Pena 'The Fifty-billion dollar man'

You might be thinking, "Does that mean I have to cut out all of my friends?" In some cases, yes. You can still be a good friend for the people you care about, but if they are self-destructive, you might take on their same self-defeating traits by being around them all the time. It's more about having boundaries around when you want to answer phone calls/emails/messages. If they are people you see every day, and there is nothing you can do about it, then you need to consider moving into an environment that is more suitable for growth. Some successful people advise one to cut off everyone that does not support them, change their phone number and avoid contact from everyone that has no relationship with their end goals. The reasoning is that these people are merely a counter-productive distraction.

Part of the meditative experience can include pondering around the relationship we share with everything in our life, from the closest relationships to the more subtle ones. What can be optimized? Can you improve your sleeping environment? Try blacking out the windows and having nature/rain audio tracks from YouTube playing in the background while you sleep. Always embrace the benefits that come from the good and bad within your life. Let the negativity accelerate you and function as a teacher.

Believe

"Those who think they can and those who think they can't usually are both right." – Confucius

The victories we have in our life all start in our mind. We set out to reach a target, follow our vision, plan, and execute on our goals. Many of us are defeated by our minds before we even get started. We allow limiting beliefs to paralyze us from taking action.

* * *

"Do just once what others say you can't do, and you will never pay attention to their limitations again." – James Cook

Think deeply, what is it about yourself that you feel holding you back? In reality, you can do anything imaginable as long as it doesn't violate the laws of physics. Some would argue that even that is debatable!

One of the most common beliefs is, "I can't do this because of x,y,z." Definitive statements like this stop us from further progression. A reframe of this statement would look like this, "I can do this if I..." and then the mind starts looking for solutions and reasons behind how and why you can succeed.

* * *

Exercise as if your life depends on it - because it does!

As we spoke about earlier, in the power of keystone habits, having an exercise regimen will positively influence many facets of one's life. From eating well to consistently meeting positive and inspired people. High-intensity interval training (HIIT) has been shown to provide a vast array of benefits, from the release of feel-good chemicals to weight loss, and even improvements in brain function and memory. Perhaps the most important advantage that comes from exercising consistently is that it helps to prevent neurodegenerative conditions such as Dementia and Alzheimers. Working out helps with depression and anxiety. Some studies also speculate that working out provides us with anti-aging properties. In our cells we have telomeres. They are protein caps located at the end of our chromosomes and are supposably markers of aging and overall health. As we get older our telomeres shrink. Working out helps add a protective layer to the telomeres, in turn, slowing down the aging process.

How to work out with or without a gym

You do not need a gym membership to start getting into shape and reaping the mental benefits that come with working out. After all, gyms are a modern invention. Body weight training can be an intensive way to work out. The reason body weight exercises are so powerful is that they contribute to our "functional strength." When we work out using machines at the gym, only a select few muscles are being worked on in many cases.

Body weight training, however, enables multiple muscle groups to receive work out simultaneously. Often people who are new to working out spend too much time on the machines and many of their muscles are neglected leaving them more prone to injuries.

13 Silence

"All men's miseries derive from not being able to sit in a quiet room alone."

– Blaise Pascal

Many of our answers are within ourselves. One of the detrimental effects that come with the information age is that we are looking outside of ourselves and passing over our authority to external forces. Often we look to others to determine what a good life path looks like.

"If you don't have a plan, you become part of somebody else's plan."
– Terence McKenna

We are all built differently, so it's essential to have a close relationship with our intuition. Our creativity can find more freedom when we are less under the subconscious influence of others.

It's important now and then to detach from the overstimulation that comes from 21st century living. Now and then, spend some time in nature away from the noise of the loud cities and experience the inner peace that comes with relaxing in nature or the wilderness.

* * *

"And most important, dare to follow your heart and intuition. They somehow already know what you truly want to become. Everything else is secondary." – Steve Jobs

Silence is a Teacher

While analyzing the spaces between our thoughts, we are able to become conscious of what our mind yearns to consider. A higher level of awareness arises as we become more aware of our immediate impulses as our thoughts pass through us. Boredom ignites original thoughts; social media tends to condition us to look to others for stimulation and even emotional management – enough that we lose our ability to be alone with ourselves. We lose the capacity to relate with ourselves. Personal discovery aligns us with our intuitions. No harm comes from boredom if accepted with an open mind. Boredom evokes reflection. It is within this reflection that we can determine what is meaningful to us.

Becoming successful can often be a lonely process. If you were to look back three years from where you are at today, after accruing success, you would reflect at these times where you would see these bored moments as catalysts for meaningful decisions and change. Think back to when you were a kid, how vivid your imagination was. Being alone in a room with just a pen and paper was enough for you to create another universe for yourself. The feeling of enchantment and awe is something that never goes away. It is something you can tap into at any time if you want to.

* * *

Boredom is never a negative thing. Procrastination, on the other hand, is something else. It's fear that is causing inaction. The silence of boredom is something to be embraced. Albert Einstein lived in an age where there were no computers, left with letters/papers to communicate with peers; scientists would be delayed sending out letters/papers around the world. Much of his conclusions were drawn from within, tapping into his creativity and mental resources. Without boredom, would Einstein have tested his curiosities to the point of developing the theories of relativity? Unfortunately, due to the hyper-stimulating age, we live in, people do their best to avoid boredom by engaging in forms of instant gratification – because of this, the genius that lives within many will not be experienced or expressed. Procrastination is a self-inflicted behavior. We all have the ability to do the bare minimum of a task to at least get started. However, our mind comes up with reasons as to why we can't do something no matter how untrue. In a sense procrastination doesn't exist, it's a label for not starting. The key is to bypass the thoughts that cause us to do the things we know we shouldn't be doing. Procrastination can be transcended if we take the simple step of planning even if its brief. The mere act of planning can build momentum and prevent wasted days. If you can judge your actions as learning experiences, then you will become more and more satisfied with your efforts. As many of us know, once we get started everything gets easier. The fear of failure can be powerful and cause paralysis by analysis. A powerful means of overcoming this is to view getting started as not something we either succeed or fail in, but as experiments. It is the micro experiments and planning that we persist on in spite of setbacks that will take us to the next level.

Bring into awareness what it is that is holding you back. Is it money? Is it lack of knowledge? Is it fear? Start to look at the problems you face and if it is fear, try to do one thing each day that counters the fear. If it's money, try to do something on a lower scale within your budget – think minimum viable products. You might have an app you want to produce and believe that it will cost half a million to build. Start with making a one thousand dollar app and then work from there. By addressing each fear, or doubt that crosses your mind with a mentality of overcoming these kinds of negative noises you will find a way out, a way to make progress despite the perceived negative limitations.

The next enemy we face is perfectionism, which stops us from ever starting. In reality, nothing and nobody is perfect. The concept of perfection is merely an idea or theory. The only thing that can perfectly happen is that you learn, fail, and then start again – In doing this, you get a firmer grasp on reality and come into closer alignment with your goals. Never think that it is an embarrassment to fail. In reality, you will grow through all of these processes. There is no other choice – Just start!

Social media is a marketing tool. It can provide you with access to a world of people with talents that you otherwise would have never met. The power of social media can be understood when we become aware as to whether we are marketing or being marketed to. The social media era that we find ourselves in today is not giving people time to really experience and sit with their emotions since many of us are distracted, multitasking, and seeking out validation from others. Many people are living their lives in a way where they are living for a better image instead of a better life. It takes time to notice the distinction between the two as they can seem like the same thing. The ego often feels like the self and has its emotional desires. Social media seems to be bridging the line between the two in a very subtle way. As a result, more and more people are being diagnosed with mental disorders because they have become too preoccupied with their image instead of focusing on their life.

* * *

A balanced life comes from building the parts of yourself that matter, not just the superficial elements. Many of the entrepreneurs that people aspire to be enjoyed living in an era that was less polluted by social media where they had a healthier relationship with their purpose. People need to define for themselves whether social media is supporting their goals or not.

The Smoke Screen of Security

A lot of us want security; many people would rather be secure and unhappy than to have to face uncertainty. There is no cookie cutter response when determining whether a full-time job versus being an entrepreneur is in one's best interests. We all have limitations when it comes to tolerating stress. At the same time, it is rare for corporate 9 to

5 jobs to provide its employees with 5 or 10 year contracts. It is safer in many respects to go after your dreams as you will fail by default if you never actually try. Security comes from learning so much and developing a skill set that makes you indispensable. If you are working for yourself, then efforts need to be dedicated to learning, reinvesting in yourself, and building a network. If you are trying to generate security within an organization, then the goal is to fit the requirements of the people in charge of you. A vital question one needs to ask themselves is; who are you trying to build security for?

Your Network

There comes a time in life where you need to weigh up who are the real assets in your life. This can be a grieving process because you may have to address the friendships in your life that are ultimately self-destructive. Just like in Autumn, leaves need to fall for new ones to grow. View your network as your account. Your account is the result of what comes in and what comes out. Do you have friends that consistently take more from you than they give? It is a personal responsibility to ensure that your network benefits you and that your account, emotionally, is positive. If your account is ignored, not only can you fall into negativity, but you can also become a liability for the people around you that have positive accounts. Ensure that you are surrounding yourself with people that are on a similar mission to you or at the place that you want to be. It is often better to be alone than to be surrounded by the wrong people. Group thought can be negative;

if you can step away from the mainstream or mediocre, you will be more likely to attract the type of person that will lift you. The interesting thing about building a positive network that accelerates your growth is that it will never be a simple process. The people that you will meet in life that will lift you will often be met outside of your comfort zone. This could include being at the social events you never go to, or the bars you don't attend. Your task is to put yourself in these environments even if it is uncomfortable. This could mean having a coffee in a high-end hotel lobby or going to a networking event even if you feel anxious expressing yourself. The good news is, it gets easier and easier with practice. Confidence is often referred to as situational confidence. When you become accustomed to situations that used to make you feel anxious, but you now know how to handle yourself, the anxiety subsides. When having the aspirations of building a powerful network of high achievers, it is important to avoid the negative energies that drag you down as they too will affect your vibe – which in short means that we need to take responsibility for the vibe we put out for the rest of the world.

Accountability and the Power of Words

The biggest amount of time wasted in your life is likely going to be a result of not committing to the things you said you are going to do. This can include the promises you make to yourself. Words are incredibly powerful and should be treated with the utmost respect. Words can be used to manipulate or sell people on a concept or image, but the worst thing one can do to themselves is to use their own words against themselves. Some people get so used to selling to other people that they eventually sell themselves out; they become deluded by their lies or tactics used for skewing reality. If you have no accountability, how do you measure your progress? If we say we are going to the gym, then we have to do it. If we can't stick to our word, how do we believe ourselves when we are setting grander goals in the future. If you have neglected your commitments in the past and have problems believing that you will change. Keep things simple. Let's say you want to go to the gym. Set a simple goal. Write down, *This Wednesday and Friday I will go to the gym.* Once you do it, tick it off, and by sticking to your word, you will begin to gain confidence and self-belief around the goals you set going forward.

* * *

Our word is our bond with the universe. We need to respect it and take our commitments and promises with ourselves very seriously, or we are wasting our time, energy, and even integrity. Its normal for us to be quick to judge others, but unfortunately, we are also quick to justify not following through on the thing we say we will do. When we set out to complete our commitments, break the goal down and figure out the commitments between that are necessary to get to where we want to be. The power of words is something that people tend to misunderstand and under-appreciate. Our words have more power than we think and believe. Words are responsible for all of the good and bad in the world, from signifying marriages, to starting world wars. The accountability of word is one of our biggest assets because if we don’t understand the tremendous potential energy behind words, we miss out on its ability to magnify our life into another place, whether that's externally or internally. By knowing who you are, and being strict with your word you will get to where you want to be because you will be adamant with yourself around what you say and what you do.

Just Ask

One of the key concepts that people overlook in life is the exchanges that take place around us. Sometimes it is in the subtlest of ways. When we are at the shop and need to buy something, even going through the checkout, we are still asking permission in the subtlest of ways at times. As entrepreneurs, we need to be willing to ask. If we don't ask, we get nothing. If we do ask, we infinitely increase the chances of getting something – and that something potentially being what we want. Rejection is a part of life that is often required when creating success. The art of asking comes from removing the emotional part and being free from the outcomes and seeing it as an inevitable part of the process when moving towards success. When you want something, be precise in what you ask for. Don't ask for less than you want because you are expecting a no. Being entitled and having the expectations for more in life is normal. When you are making deals, if you ask for too little, you might end up resentful knowing that you could have or should have received more.

There is a story of a homeless man who sees a

worker each day coming out for coffee. For three days in a row, he asks the worker for a dollar. Each time, it's at an inconvenient time, and the worker is not carrying a dollar on him. On the 4th day he asks again, "Hey do you have a dollar." The man pulls out a bunch of money, "So you want a dollar?" He gives him a dollar and says, "You could have had more, but you only asked for a dollar." Don't get a dollar when you can get a hundred. Getting what we are worth stems from being able to ask for what it is we want without being afraid.

Comfort Zone

Comfort is a false concept. It is a repetition of feeling we have felt before. People tend to look as discomfort as something that is negative, but growth is done outside of our comfort zone. Being in a state of perpetually acclimating to new circumstances is what grows us. Discomfort provides us with thoughts and adrenaline which lead us towards action. It brings on instinctual behaviors that would not come into existence when we are in a stable and secure environment. Discomfort brings out our strength and fuel for creating greatness. Discomfort can be broken down to disabling-comfort. In doing this, we gain insight into how we can structure our plans to push past our usual limitations. To get something we have never had before we must do something we have never done before. Aspire for comfort but disable it to push for more. Feeling comfortable is a false sense of security that causes our creativity, strength, and focus to atrophy. If you have a new idea or goal, don't let the idea die inside of you, where you forget about it and move onto something else. Break the idea down and put tiny steps in place over the next week to get things moving. Think of ideas as plants. You can buy a plant that already has soil and flowers growing – you can water the plant, watch it grow and become more beautiful, or you can look at it and let it slowly die. We can let our ideas die, or we can nurture our ideas so that we stay excited. The action keeps our ideas alive and lets them flourish into real-world beauty.

14 Embrace Boredom

Perhaps you don't know where to start? You might be thinking, "I don't have any passions. I'm bored. I don't know what to do with my life." Being bored is not a bad thing. It's an emotional state that allows for deeper levels of introspection. Before you distract yourself with your Facebook and Instagram, sit in the boredom and listen to your heart. You will eventually gravitate to the things you care about. Embracing boredom and sitting in silence will give you time to think. Go back to when you were fourteen, or when you were eight, what was something that you were naturally drawn to? Not everything in life can be monetized. Not everyone has a passion that can be converted into a full-time living. However, in this day and age, it is more possible than one would expect. There has never been a better time in human history to control your destiny. The internet gives everyone the opportunity and possibility of putting work on display for the rest of the world to see. If you have a hobby that excites you, you could film yourself demonstrating your mastery and even creating a course around your passion. Your passions are valuable, and just by starting small, in the long term, big things can happen.

* * *

Burn the Bridges

Cut off all other possibilities but success. When we burn the bridges, we force ourselves to succeed and find the solution. Having a backup plan is great, but the downside of backup plans is that we are also attracting the failed scenario where we manifest the backup plan the same way visualization helps us when manifesting success. If you are half-heartedly committed to your business, your results will be weaker than if you have put everything on the line, and you are in a situation where you will force yourself to do nothing but strive for success.

15 Habits

"The chains of habit are too light to be felt until they are too heavy to be broken." – Warren Buffett

The defining factor that separates the winners from the rest are habits. Habits and consistency are foundational when achieving mastery in any field. Our habits are usually the critical feature behind our successes and failures in life. It's what separates the 1% from the 99%. The decisions and habits we take part in on a daily basis are responsible for whether we get on an upward spiral in life or a downward spiral. Many of the little choices and habits we take part in having a compounding effect over the long term. Because the power of our habits is so strong, it's important to understand how they work and become more conscious around which habits are supporting you and which ones are holding you back as subtle as they may be.

What Exactly are Habits?

Habits are the activities and processes we take part in on a consistent basis. Many of these processes are automatic for us. You may have heard the saying, "Humans are creatures of habit."

There is truth to this. Our unconscious mind likes when we are operating on autopilot since less mental energy is used. This natural tendency can benefit us when we cultivate great habits especially when success also becomes habitual.

Eliminate Bad Habits and Cultivate Stronger Ones

It can be quite challenging taking up a new habit particularly one that seems to deplete our sense of will power. Neuroscientists tend to say that it takes 66 days on average to fully integrate a new habit. When aiming to eliminate a bad habit, getting to the *why* can be useful, paying attention to the triggers and patterns that lead us to succumb to self-destructive tendencies broadens our awareness and protects us from making bad choices. Whatever it is that makes you cause you to feel sucked into bad behavior patterns, choose to do things differently next time you feel stuck. When things get rough for you, instead of drinking alcohol, go for a run. A decision like this could potentially save you weeks or months of heartache. Going for a run can potentially detach you from your negative emotions and give you a clearer and objective grasp on reality. Drinking could bring you straight into a downward spiral and potentially an addiction. When we avoid our problems, they often taunt us until we accept them. Things can get bad and at the moment, things can often feel too heavy, as if our problems are something we can't move past – time heals, often faster than we think it will. Going for a run when things get bad can give us more perspective and save us from future suffering.

* * *

The Structure of Habits

The acting out a habit has a defined structure. Consider the following:

Cue —> Action —> Reward

The cue is what triggers us to take part in the habit. For instance, if it is social media, the cue that triggers one to check their social media is a feeling of loneliness. The action of checking social media is complemented with a feeling of reward that comes in the form of a message or notification. Analyzing the cues that trigger our habits and implementing healthy rewards for positive habits is vital. A habit or activity that is healthy is one that is rewarding – we enjoy participating in the activity because it puts us in the *flow state*.

16 It's the "Sizzle" not the product!

As CEO and founder of *MYCOMEUP.com* – a social platform matching and connecting entrepreneurs, freelancers and creatives looking to do more than date – every day whenever I'm online or I check my inbox, I'm constantly met with the same question by aspiring and early-stage entrepreneurs: "What's the best market to start my business in?", "I can't come up with a business idea", or most common, "How do I protect my idea?". This something I feel many aspiring entrepreneurs spend too much time thinking about, or in some cases end up procrastinating over, and never end up starting their business because of it. Over the past few years, the internet has birthed a series of billion dollar ideas and exposed a number of money-making business opportunities that require no entry barriers. We have watched the likes of Mark Zuckerberg build a startup from his dorm room into one of the world's most successful tech companies in the world. Their stories are amazing and there have been millions more since, however, this has not changed the customer's demands or expectations. Customers, clients, and consumers all still require the same thing: quality, convenience, and a good deal. Many of us are still caught up with coming up with the next big thing when in reality that isn't the only way to create a successful business. In fact businesses and industries that already exist provide a roadmap and market value that you can automatically tap into. There is no such thing as a customer that spends their whole life buying from one brand! Why? Because other brands can simply come into the same market space with the same product but a different sales proposition. You see, the customer may be comfortable with the brands they already use, but if you can make your product *sizzle* you'll be sure to get their attention!

I remember my first entrepreneurial endeavor back when I was 15 years old and still in secondary school. At the top of our schoolyard, there was a football pitch where all of the boys in my year would play football, and I noticed that at the end of our break they would come off the pitch hot, sweaty, and thirsty. I used to come into school with a drink my mum would pack for me and noticed that if I sold it at the end of the break when everyone finished playing football I could sell what was once a 50p drink for £1.00! That's right, double. I would only have one but everyone would bid and fight to buy it from me. So, a few days later, just outside my school gates, there was a shop selling one pack of Coca-Cola for £2.50 – buy one get one free – which in return got me 8 drinks. I went home with them after school and kept them in the fridge overnight. The next day, I came in with my bag dripping from the ice cold drinks. When the school bell rang this time I yelled, "I have ice cold drinks!", and in seconds each sold for a £1.00, making me £5.50 profit! You see, the school also sold drinks, however there were two problems; firstly, you had to go to the school shop and line up to buy one, and secondly by the time the school bell rang and everyone had to stop playing football the shop closed! So what made my product better? The convenience. I would be right there as they finished playing so they didn't have to cue up. The *quality* of the drink would be nice and cold by the time they got them and as for *the deal,* I could have charged them more but I didn't! This is a prime example that reveals that your product doesn't have to be new or the first of its kind, as long as you can brand and market yourself, your company, or product, you will be able to attract and tap into a world of prospects looking for convenience, value and quality.

17 Don't be afraid to start!

Start now or start as soon as you can. The sooner you start, the better. The quicker you come to terms with your life situation, the quicker you start making positive changes for the better. The concept of starting is based around whether we do it or not. Never be afraid of starting. The school system and our upbringing teach us that we have to research to find our solutions. In reality, sometimes the research is in the result of our doings. When getting a business off the ground, there is no set in stone structure, no road map to follow. It's about testing and experimenting. This is what guides our next step and determines the structure of our solutions. We don't know what solution we are supposed to be searching for until we start.

A friend of mine grew up in a strict household where there was a weight of expectation on her shoulders, at an early age to become a doctor or a lawyer. Deep down she wanted to be an artist, so this emotional conflict made life harder than it was.

Eventually, she got married and traveled the world with her partner. She was able to stay in hostels for free in exchange for her lovely painting services. However, when she got back from traveling, she got sucked back into the monotony of 9 to 5 life and the pressures and expectations of the people around her. She eventually found herself depressed again because she stopped drawing. If there is a creative force inside of you, it needs to be expressed. It is essential to transcend or avoid the powers that tell you to quit your passion and join the rat race. If you are an artist, it is usually a tough thing to monetize. It's worth having a job/trade so that you can survive until you can turn your artwork into money. The key is never to neglect your heart's passion because eventually this negligence can lead to feeling more stressed and unfulfilled. Detach from the ideas that social pressure places as to what is the right or wrong path. Everyone needs to decide what is right for them. This is something that only you can answer. Step into the unknown and be willing to follow your passions.

If you want to start a business, put a little bit of money aside and build a website. It's very easy these days – *SquareSpace.com* makes it very easy to get started (for about 10 dollars you can have a website up in less than a few hours). Take action so that the universe and world can take your dreams more seriously and you can come into alignment with your destiny. Don't worry about the things you don't have. Focus on what you do have. You have yourself! Just start. Don't be afraid of failure, as cliché as it sounds. Fear of failing and the fear of getting started are among the biggest problems that most people with an entrepreneurial spirit face. Unfortunately, the concept of failure is emotionally powerful. As we are dragged through the educational system, we are taught to view failure as something that is negative and which equates to adverse life outcomes. In the real world, failure is one of the most potent tools that bless us with practical information which helps us to create success later on.

In memory of Edward Sekyonda.

Thank you Anita Kironde Musisi (mom).

Printed in Great Britain
by Amazon

61914364R00081